Enhancing Quality Through Re-engineering: A Practical Guide for Improvement

Strategies, Techniques, and Case Studies for Transforming Processes and Achieving Excellence

By

Priscilla Knox

TABLE OF CONTENTS

INTRODUCTION

Welcome to "Enhancing Quality Through Re-engineering: A Practical Guide for Improvement." In today's rapidly evolving business landscape, organizations are constantly challenged to adapt and innovate to stay competitive. One key aspect of this adaptation is the pursuit of quality enhancement, which plays a vital role in ensuring customer satisfaction, operational efficiency, and overall success.

This practical guide aims to provide you with a comprehensive framework for enhancing quality through the process of re-engineering. Before delving into the specifics of Re-engineering and its application to quality improvement, let's first explore the foundational concepts underlying this endeavor.

Understanding the Concept of Re-engineering

Re-engineering, also known as business process Re-engineering (BPR), is a fundamental restructuring of an organization's processes, systems, and workflows to achieve significant improvements in performance, efficiency, and effectiveness. Unlike incremental improvements or optimization efforts, Re-engineering involves a radical redesign of existing processes, often resulting in dramatic changes to the way work is performed.

The concept of Re-engineering emerged in the early 1990s, popularized by Michael Hammer and James Champy in their groundbreaking book, "Re-engineering the Corporation." At its core, Re-engineering challenges organizations to question the status quo and break free from traditional ways of operating. It encourages a shift from a focus on tasks and functions to a focus on end-to-end processes, with the ultimate goal of delivering greater value to customers and stakeholders.

Re-engineering is not merely about automating or digitizing existing processes; it requires a holistic approach that encompasses people, technology, and organizational culture. It involves rethinking every aspect of how work is done, from customer interactions to back-office operations, with an emphasis on simplicity, speed, and customer-centricity.

Importance of Quality Enhancement

Quality enhancement is a critical objective for organizations across industries, as it directly impacts customer satisfaction, brand reputation, and long-term success. In today's hyper-connected world, where customer expectations are constantly evolving, maintaining high standards of quality is essential for sustaining competitiveness.

Quality enhancement encompasses various dimensions, including product quality, service quality, and process quality. It involves not only meeting but exceeding customer expectations by consistently delivering products and services that are reliable, durable, and meet or exceed specifications.

By enhancing quality, organizations can achieve several key benefits, including:

Improved customer satisfaction and loyalty: High-quality products and services lead to satisfied customers who are more likely to remain loyal and recommend the organization to others.

Enhanced reputation and brand value: A reputation for quality excellence can differentiate an organization from its competitors and attract new customers.

Increased operational efficiency: Quality improvement often leads to streamlined processes, reduced waste, and lower costs.

Regulatory compliance and risk mitigation: Meeting quality standards and regulations helps organizations avoid costly fines, legal issues, and reputational damage.

In today's dynamic business environment, where disruption is the norm, quality enhancement is not just a one-time initiative but an ongoing commitment to continuous improvement.

Overview of the Practical Guide

This practical guide is designed to equip you with the knowledge, tools, and strategies needed to enhance quality through Re-engineering. Whether you're a business leader, manager, consultant, or quality professional, the insights and methodologies presented in this guide can help you drive meaningful change and achieve sustainable results.

The guide is structured as follows:

Foundations of Quality: This section lays the groundwork by exploring the concept of quality in a business context, tracing its historical evolution, and examining modern quality frameworks and standards.

The Re-engineering Approach: Here, we delve into the principles of Re-engineering, outlining its key components and demonstrating how it can be integrated with quality enhancement initiatives.

Assessment and Analysis: This section focuses on evaluating current processes and identifying opportunities for improvement through rigorous assessment and analysis.

Visioning and Planning: Setting clear objectives and developing a strategic plan are essential for successful Re-engineering efforts. This section provides practical guidance on creating a vision for quality enhancement and devising a roadmap for implementation.

Process Redesign: The heart of Re-engineering lies in redesigning core business processes to achieve optimal performance. This section explores best practices and methodologies for process redesign.

Technology Integration: Leveraging technology is often a key enabler of Re-engineering initiatives. Here, we discuss how organizations can harness the power of technology to enhance quality and drive innovation.

Change Management: Effective change management is critical for overcoming resistance and ensuring successful implementation. This section provides insights into managing the human side of Re-engineering.

Continuous Improvement: Continuous improvement is the cornerstone of quality excellence. This section explores strategies for fostering a culture of continuous learning and improvement.

Case Studies: Real-world examples of successful Re-engineering projects provide valuable insights and inspiration for readers.

Future Trends and Considerations: Finally, we look ahead to emerging trends in quality management and Re-engineering, offering insights into future opportunities and challenges.

Each section of the guide is packed with practical tips, tools, and case studies to help you apply the concepts discussed to your organization's unique context. Whether you're embarking on your first Re-engineering project or seeking to optimize existing processes, this guide will serve as a valuable resource on your journey toward enhancing quality and driving organizational excellence.

In the following chapters, we will delve deeper into each aspect of Re-engineering and quality enhancement, providing actionable guidance and best practices to help you achieve your goals. Let's embark on this journey together, as we explore the transformative power of Re-engineering in enhancing quality and driving organizational success.

This introduction sets the stage for the rest of the practical guide, providing readers with a clear understanding of the concepts of Re-engineering, quality enhancement, and the structure of the guide itself.

Priscilla Knox

CHAPTER 1:

Foundations of Quality

Quality is a multifaceted concept that lies at the heart of organizational success. In this section, we will explore the foundational principles of quality, including its definition in a business context, historical perspectives on quality management, and the evolution of modern quality frameworks and standards.

1.1 Defining Quality in a Business Context

Quality can be defined as the degree to which a product, service, or process meets or exceeds customer expectations and requirements. It encompasses various dimensions, including performance, reliability, durability, and conformance to specifications. In a business context, quality is not merely about meeting minimum standards but striving for excellence in all aspects of operations.

At its core, quality is about delivering value to customers and stakeholders. It involves understanding their needs, preferences, and priorities and aligning organizational efforts to consistently meet or exceed their expectations. Quality is not a static attribute but a dynamic concept that evolves in response to changing market dynamics, technological advancements, and customer feedback.

1.2 Historical Perspectives on Quality Management

The pursuit of quality is not a new phenomenon but has deep roots in human history. Throughout the ages, civilizations have recognized the importance of quality in craftsmanship, trade, and commerce. Ancient civilizations such as the Egyptians, Greeks, and Romans had rudimentary systems for ensuring quality in the production of goods and services.

However, it was during the Industrial Revolution of the 18th and 19th centuries that the modern concept of quality management began to take shape. The advent of mass production brought with its new challenges related to consistency, reliability, and standardization. Pioneers such as Frederick Winslow Taylor, Henry Ford, and Walter Shewhart laid the groundwork for modern quality management principles through their work on scientific management, assembly line production, and statistical process control.

The mid-20th century saw the emergence of quality management as a distinct discipline, thanks in large part to the contributions of quality gurus such as W. Edwards Deming, Joseph M. Juran, and Armand V. Feigenbaum. These thought leaders emphasized the importance of a systematic approach to quality improvement, statistical analysis, and the involvement of management and employees in the pursuit of quality excellence.

1.3 Modern Quality Frameworks and Standards

In today's globalized economy, organizations rely on established quality frameworks and standards to guide their quality management efforts. These frameworks provide a structured approach to quality improvement and serve as a benchmark for evaluating organizational performance. Some of the most widely recognized quality frameworks and standards include:

ISO 9000 series: The International Organization for Standardization (ISO) 9000 series provides a set of quality management standards that help organizations establish, implement, and maintain effective quality management systems (QMS). ISO 9001, the most well-known standard in the series, outlines requirements for QMS certification and is used by organizations around the world to demonstrate their commitment to quality.

Total Quality Management (TQM): TQM is a management philosophy that emphasizes continuous improvement, customer focus, and employee involvement in quality management. Developed in the 1980s and popularized by quality gurus such as

Deming and Juran, TQM advocates for a holistic approach to quality improvement that involves all levels of the organization.

Six Sigma: Six Sigma is a data-driven methodology for process improvement that aims to reduce defects and variability in manufacturing and service processes. Originally developed by Motorola in the 1980s and later popularized by companies like General Electric, Six Sigma utilizes statistical tools and techniques to identify and eliminate root causes of quality problems.

Lean Manufacturing: Lean manufacturing, also known as Lean production or simply Lean, is a systematic approach to minimizing waste and maximizing value in manufacturing processes. Originating from the Toyota Production System (TPS) in the 1950s, Lean principles have been widely adopted across industries to improve efficiency, quality, and customer satisfaction.

Agile and Lean-Agile: In the realm of software development and project management, Agile methodologies such as Scrum and Kanban promote iterative development, collaboration, and adaptability to change. Similarly, Lean-Agile frameworks like SAFe (Scaled Agile Framework) combine Lean principles with Agile practices to enable large-scale Agile transformations in complex organizations.

These modern quality frameworks and standards provide organizations with the tools and methodologies needed to drive continuous improvement, enhance customer satisfaction, and achieve operational excellence. By embracing these frameworks and standards, organizations can establish a culture of quality and position themselves for long-term success in today's competitive marketplace.

This section lays the groundwork for understanding quality management principles, tracing their historical development, and exploring the contemporary frameworks and standards that guide organizations in their pursuit of quality excellence.

CHAPTER 2:

The Re-engineering Approach

Re-engineering, also known as business process Re-engineering (BPR), is a strategic approach to organizational change that aims to achieve dramatic improvements in performance, efficiency, and effectiveness. In this section, we will explore the principles of Re-engineering, the key components of the Re-engineering process, and how Re-engineering can be integrated with quality enhancement initiatives to drive organizational excellence.

2.1 Principles of Re-engineering

At its core, Re-engineering is guided by several key principles that distinguish it from other change management approaches. These principles include:

Radical Redesign: Re-engineering involves a radical redesign of existing processes, systems, and workflows, rather than incremental improvements or optimization efforts. It challenges organizations to question the status quo and re-imagine how work is done from the ground up.

End-to-End Perspective: Re-engineering takes an end-to-end perspective on processes, focusing on the entire value chain rather than individual tasks or functions. It seeks to streamline and simplify processes to eliminate unnecessary steps and handoffs.

Customer-centricity: Re-engineering is driven by a relentless focus on meeting customer needs and expectations. It aims to deliver products and services that provide value to customers and enhance their overall experience.

Cross-Functional Collaboration: Re-engineering requires collaboration across functional boundaries, bringing together people from different parts of the organization to work towards common goals. It emphasizes teamwork, communication, and shared accountability for outcomes.

Use of Technology: Re-engineering leverages technology as an enabler of change, enabling organizations to automate, digitize, and optimize processes for greater efficiency and effectiveness. It explores innovative technologies such as artificial intelligence, robotic process automation, and data analytics to drive process improvement.

Performance Measurement: Re-engineering emphasizes the importance of performance measurement and accountability. It establishes clear metrics and key performance indicators (KPIs) to track progress towards goals and identify areas for further improvement.

By adhering to these principles, organizations can embark on successful Re-engineering initiatives that deliver tangible results and drive sustainable change.

2.2 Key Components of the Re-engineering Process

The Re-engineering process typically consists of several key components that guide organizations through the journey of transformation. These components may vary depending on the specific context and objectives of the Re-engineering initiative, but generally include:

Identification of Opportunities: The first step in the Re-engineering process is to identify opportunities for improvement. This may involve conducting process audits, analyzing performance data, and soliciting feedback from stakeholders to identify pain points and areas of inefficiency.

Visioning and Goal Setting: Once opportunities for improvement have been identified, the next step is to create a vision for the future state of the organization. This involves setting clear objectives, defining success criteria, and articulating a compelling vision that motivates stakeholders to embrace change.

Process Analysis and Redesign: With a clear vision in place, organizations can begin the process of analyzing and redesigning core business processes. This may involve mapping current processes, identifying bottlenecks and inefficiencies, and designing new workflows that align with organizational goals and objectives.

Technology Integration: Technology plays a crucial role in enabling Re-engineering efforts. Organizations must carefully evaluate and select the right technology solutions to support their redesigned processes, whether it be implementing new software systems, automating manual tasks, or leveraging data analytics to drive decision-making.

Change Management: Re-engineering initiatives often encounter resistance from employees who are accustomed to existing ways of working. Effective change management is essential for overcoming resistance and ensuring buy-in from all stakeholders. This may involve communication, training, and providing support to help employees adapt to new ways of working.

Implementation and Monitoring: Once the redesigned processes have been finalized, it's time to implement them in the organization.

This may involve piloting new processes, training employees, and gradually rolling out changes across the organization. It's important to closely monitor progress and adjust course as needed to ensure that the Re-engineering initiative stays on track.

Continuous Improvement: Re-engineering is not a one-time event but an ongoing journey of continuous improvement. Organizations must establish mechanisms for monitoring performance, soliciting feedback, and iterating on their processes to ensure that they remain aligned with evolving business needs and customer expectations.

By addressing these key components, organizations can effectively navigate the Re-engineering process and achieve meaningful improvements in performance, efficiency, and quality.

2.3 Integrating Re-engineering with Quality Enhancement

Re-engineering and quality enhancement are closely intertwined concepts that share a common goal of driving organizational excellence. By integrating Re-engineering with quality enhancement initiatives, organizations can leverage the strengths of both approaches to achieve synergistic outcomes.

One way to integrate Re-engineering with quality enhancement is to embed quality principles and methodologies into the Re-engineering process itself. For example, organizations can apply tools and techniques from quality management frameworks such as Six Sigma, Lean, and Total Quality Management (TQM) to identify and eliminate defects, reduce waste, and improve process efficiency.

Similarly, Re-engineering efforts can be guided by a customer-centric approach that prioritizes quality and customer satisfaction. By understanding customer needs and preferences, organizations can redesign processes to deliver products and services that consistently meet or exceed customer expectations.

Additionally, technology plays a crucial role in both Re-engineering and quality enhancement efforts. Organizations can leverage technology solutions such as enterprise resource planning (ERP) systems, customer relationship management (CRM) software, and business intelligence tools to streamline processes, improve data visibility, and enhance decision-making capabilities.

Finally, effective change management is essential for integrating Re-engineering with quality enhancement initiatives. Organizations must communicate the rationale for change, involve stakeholders in the decision-making process, and provide the necessary support and resources to facilitate a smooth transition.

By integrating Re-engineering with quality enhancement initiatives, organizations can achieve transformative results that drive sustainable growth, competitive advantage, and customer satisfaction.

This section provides an overview of the Re-engineering approach, including its principles, key components, and integration with quality enhancement initiatives. It sets the stage for the practical application of Re-engineering principles to enhance quality and drive organizational improvement.

Priscilla Knox

CHAPTER 3:

Assessment and Analysis

Assessment and analysis are critical components of the Re-engineering process, providing organizations with valuable insights into their current state and identifying opportunities for improvement. In this section, we will explore the importance of evaluating current processes and practices, methods for identifying gaps and opportunities for improvement, and various tools and techniques for analysis.

3.1 Evaluating Current Processes and Practices

Before embarking on a Re-engineering initiative, organizations need to conduct a comprehensive assessment of their current processes and practices. This involves evaluating existing workflows, systems, and procedures to identify strengths, weaknesses, and areas for improvement. Some common methods for evaluating current processes include:

Process Mapping: Process mapping involves visually representing the sequence of steps involved in a particular process, along with inputs, outputs, and decision points. By mapping out current processes, organizations can gain a better understanding of how work is currently being done and identify areas of inefficiency or redundancy.

Value Stream Mapping: Value stream mapping is a specific type of process mapping that focuses on identifying value-added and non-value-added activities within a process. By distinguishing between activities that contribute to the creation of value for the customer and those that do not, organizations can prioritize improvement efforts and streamline their processes.

Performance Metrics: Performance metrics provide quantitative data on various aspects of organizational performance, such as productivity, quality, and customer satisfaction. By analyzing performance metrics, organizations can identify trends, patterns, and areas of under-performance that require attention.

Stakeholder Feedback: Gathering feedback from stakeholders, including employees, customers, and suppliers, is another valuable method for evaluating current processes. Stakeholder feedback can provide insights into areas of dissatisfaction, pain points, and opportunities for improvement that may not be apparent from quantitative data alone.

By employing these methods, organizations can gain a holistic understanding of their current state and lay the foundation for successful Re-engineering efforts.

3.2 Identifying Gaps and Opportunities for Improvement

Once the current state has been assessed, the next step is to identify gaps and opportunities for improvement. This involves comparing the current state against desired outcomes, industry benchmarks, and best practices to pinpoint areas where performance falls short or where there is potential for enhancement. Some techniques for identifying gaps and opportunities include:

Gap Analysis: Gap analysis involves comparing current performance against desired performance levels to identify discrepancies or "gaps" that need to be addressed. By clearly defining performance objectives and measuring progress against these objectives, organizations can identify areas where improvement is needed.

Benchmarking: Benchmarking involves comparing organizational performance against industry peers or best-in-class organizations to identify areas of competitive advantage or areas for improvement. By studying how top performers achieve their results, organizations can identify best practices and adopt them to improve their performance.

SWOT Analysis: SWOT analysis is a strategic planning tool that helps organizations identify strengths, weaknesses, opportunities, and threats related to a particular initiative or project. By analyzing internal strengths and weaknesses and external opportunities and threats, organizations can develop strategies to leverage their strengths, mitigate weaknesses, capitalize on opportunities, and mitigate threats.

Root Cause Analysis: Root cause analysis involves identifying the underlying causes of problems or issues within a process. By digging deeper into the root causes of performance issues, organizations can develop targeted solutions that address the underlying issues rather than just treating symptoms.

By utilizing these techniques, organizations can systematically identify areas for improvement and develop targeted strategies to address them, laying the groundwork for successful Re-engineering initiatives.

3.3 Tools and Techniques for Analysis

A variety of tools and techniques are available to organizations for analyzing part of the Re-engineering process. Some common tools and techniques include:

Process Flowcharts: Process flowcharts are visual representations of a process, showing the sequence of steps involved, decision points, and flow of information or materials. Flowcharts help organizations understand the flow of work and identify areas of inefficiency or complexity.

Cause-and-Effect Diagrams (Fishbone Diagrams): Cause-and-effect diagrams, also known as Fishbone diagrams, are used to identify potential causes of a problem or issue within a process. By brainstorming potential causes and organizing them into categories, organizations can uncover root causes and develop targeted solutions.

Pareto Analysis: Pareto analysis, also known as the 80/20 rule, is a technique for prioritizing improvement efforts based on the principle that a small number of factors often account for a large percentage of the total impact. By focusing on the "vital few" factors that have the greatest impact on performance, organizations can achieve significant improvements with minimal resources.

Statistical Analysis: Statistical analysis involves using statistical techniques to analyze data and identify patterns, trends, and relationships. Statistical tools such as regression analysis, hypothesis testing, and control charts can help organizations make informed decisions and identify areas for improvement based on empirical evidence.

Surveys and Questionnaires: Surveys and questionnaires are valuable tools for gathering feedback from stakeholders and collecting data on perceptions, preferences, and experiences. Organizations can gather qualitative and quantitative data that informs decision-making and drives improvement efforts by designing well-crafted surveys and questionnaires.

By leveraging these tools and techniques, organizations can conduct rigorous analysis that informs decision-making and drives continuous improvement.

This section provides a comprehensive overview of the assessment and analysis phase of the Re-engineering process, including methods for evaluating current processes, identifying gaps and opportunities for improvement, and various tools and techniques for analysis. It lays the groundwork for subsequent phases of the Re-engineering journey, providing organizations with the insights and information needed to drive meaningful change and achieve sustainable results.

Priscilla Knox

CHAPTER 4:

Visioning and Planning

Visioning and planning are crucial stages in the Re-engineering process, providing organizations with a roadmap for achieving their quality enhancement goals. In this section, we will explore the importance of setting clear objectives for quality enhancement, creating a vision for Re-engineering efforts, and developing a strategic implementation plan.

4.1 Setting Clear Objectives for Quality Enhancement

The first step in the visioning and planning process is to set clear objectives for quality enhancement. Objectives serve as guiding principles that define the desired outcomes of the Re-engineering initiative and provide a benchmark for measuring success. When setting objectives for quality enhancement, organizations should consider the following factors:

Specificity: Objectives should be specific and measurable, clearly articulating what the organization hopes to achieve in terms of quality improvement. Vague or ambiguous objectives can lead to confusion and make it difficult to track progress.

Relevance: Objectives should be relevant to the organization's overall goals and strategic priorities. They should align with the organization's mission, vision, and values, and contribute to its long-term success.

Achievability: Objectives should be realistic and achievable within a reasonable time-frame and with the resources available to the organization. Setting overly ambitious or unrealistic objectives can set the organization up for failure and demotivate employees.

Time-Bound: Objectives should be time-bound, with clear deadlines or milestones for achievement. This helps create a sense of urgency and accountability and ensures that progress toward the objectives is regularly monitored and evaluated.

By setting clear and actionable objectives for quality enhancement, organizations can create a shared vision for success and align their efforts toward achieving tangible outcomes.

4.2 Creating a Vision for Re-engineering Efforts

In addition to setting objectives for quality enhancement, organizations must also create a compelling vision for the Re-engineering efforts. A vision serves as a guiding beacon that inspires and motivates stakeholders to embrace change and rally behind the Re-engineering initiative. When creating a vision for Re-engineering efforts, organizations should consider the following elements:

Inspiration: A compelling vision should inspire and energize stakeholders, sparking enthusiasm and commitment to the Re-engineering initiative. It should communicate a sense of purpose and direction, highlighting the positive impact that the Re-engineering efforts will have on the organization and its stakeholders.

Clarity: A clear and concise vision is essential for ensuring that all stakeholders understand and buy into the Re-engineering initiative. It should clearly articulate the desired future state of the organization, including the goals, values, and principles that will guide the Re-engineering efforts.

Alignment: The vision should be aligned with the organization's overall mission, vision, and strategic priorities. It should reflect the organization's core values and priorities, reinforcing the connection between the Re-engineering initiative and the broader organizational objectives.

Flexibility: While the vision needs to provide a clear direction, it should also be flexible enough to adapt to changing circumstances and evolving stakeholder needs. A rigid or inflexible vision may become obsolete in the face of unforeseen challenges or opportunities.

By creating a compelling vision for Re-engineering efforts, organizations can inspire stakeholders, build momentum for change, and lay the foundation for a successful transformation journey.

4.3 Developing a Strategic Plan for Implementation

Once the objectives and vision have been established, the next step is to develop a strategic implementation plan. A strategic plan outlines the steps, resources, and timelines needed to achieve the objectives and realize the vision for the Re-engineering initiative. When developing a strategic implementation plan, organizations should consider the following elements:

Scope: The strategic plan should clearly define the scope of the Re-engineering initiative, including the processes, systems, and stakeholders that will be impacted. It should outline the boundaries of the initiative and ensure that all relevant stakeholders are included in the planning process.

Resource Allocation: The plan should identify the resources needed to support the Re-engineering efforts, including financial, human, and technological resources. It should allocate resources efficiently and effectively to ensure that the initiative stays on track and within budget.

Timeline: The plan should include a realistic timeline for implementation, with clear deadlines or milestones for key activities and deliverables. It should account for dependencies, risks, and uncertainties that may impact the timeline and build flexibility to accommodate unexpected delays or changes.

Risk Management: The plan should identify potential risks and challenges that may arise during the implementation process and outline strategies for mitigating or managing these risks. It should include contingency plans and alternative courses of action to address unforeseen obstacles.

Communication and Stakeholder Engagement: Effective communication and stakeholder engagement are essential for the success of the Re-engineering initiative. The plan should outline a communication strategy that keeps stakeholders informed and engaged throughout the implementation process, soliciting feedback and addressing concerns as they arise.

By developing a strategic implementation plan, organizations can ensure that their Re-engineering efforts are well-coordinated, effectively managed, and aligned with the objectives and vision for quality enhancement.

This section provides insights into the visioning and planning phase of the Re-engineering process, emphasizing the importance of setting clear objectives, creating a compelling vision, and developing a strategic implementation plan. It lays the groundwork for the subsequent phases of the Re-engineering journey, providing organizations with the tools and strategies needed to achieve their quality enhancement goals.

CHAPTER 5:

Process Redesign

Process redesign lies at the heart of Re-engineering efforts, offering organizations an opportunity to overhaul their core business processes and achieve significant improvements in performance, efficiency, and quality. In this section, we will explore the importance of process redesign, strategies for redesigning core business processes, and techniques for eliminating redundancies and inefficiencies to streamline workflows for optimal performance.

5.1 Redesigning Core Business Processes

Core business processes are the fundamental activities that drive value creation within an organization, spanning various functions and departments. Redesigning these processes involves re-imagining how work is done, from end to end, with a focus on simplification, speed, and customer-centricity. When redesigning core business processes, organizations should consider the following factors:

Customer Value: Start by understanding the needs and preferences of customers and stakeholders. What aspects of the current processes add value for customers? What aspects detract from value?

By focusing on delivering value to customers, organizations can prioritize improvement efforts that have the greatest impact on customer satisfaction.

End-to-end Perspective: Take an end-to-end perspective on processes, looking beyond individual tasks or functions to consider the entire value chain. Where are handoffs occurring between departments or functions? Are there opportunities to consolidate or integrate activities to streamline workflows and reduce complexity?

Simplicity and Speed: Simplify processes wherever possible to minimize complexity and reduce the risk of errors or delays. Look for opportunities to eliminate unnecessary steps, approvals, or paperwork that add time and effort without adding value. Streamline workflows to accelerate cycle times and improve responsiveness to customer needs.

Flexibility and Adaptability: Design processes that are flexible and adaptable to changing business conditions and customer requirements. Build mechanisms for feedback and iteration that allow processes to evolve in response to new information or emerging trends. Embrace a mindset of continuous improvement to drive ongoing innovation and excellence.

By redesigning core business processes with these principles in mind, organizations can achieve greater agility, efficiency, and effectiveness, enabling them to respond more quickly to market changes and deliver superior value to customers.

5.2 Eliminating Redundancies and Inefficiencies

One of the key objectives of process redesign is to eliminate redundancies and inefficiencies that impede organizational performance and hinder quality enhancement efforts. Redundancies and inefficiencies can take many forms, including:

Duplicate Activities: Identify and eliminate duplicate activities or tasks that add unnecessary time and effort to processes. Look for opportunities to consolidate or integrate similar activities to streamline workflows and reduce redundancy.

Manual Processes: Automate manual processes wherever possible to reduce the risk of errors, speed up cycle times, and free up employees to focus on more value-added activities. Leverage technology solutions such as robotic process automation (RPA), workflow automation, and artificial intelligence (AI) to automate repetitive tasks and improve process efficiency.

Bottlenecks: Identify bottlenecks or choke-points in processes that slow down throughput and limit capacity. Implement strategies to alleviate bottlenecks, such as reallocating resources, redesigning workflows, or implementing parallel processing to increase throughput and reduce cycle times.

Handoffs and Delays: Minimize handoffs and delays between departments or functions by streamlining communication channels, clarifying roles and responsibilities, and establishing clear escalation procedures. Reduce reliance on email and paper-based communication in favor of digital collaboration tools that facilitate real-time communication and collaboration.

By systematically identifying and eliminating redundancies and inefficiencies, organizations can streamline workflows, reduce waste, and improve overall process efficiency, laying the foundation for enhanced quality and performance.

5.3 Streamlining Workflows for Optimal Performance

The ultimate goal of process redesign is to streamline workflows for optimal performance, enabling organizations to achieve greater efficiency, agility, and effectiveness. Streamlining workflows involves optimizing the flow of work through the organization, from initial request to final delivery, focusing on minimizing waste, reducing cycle times, and enhancing customer satisfaction. When streamlining workflows, organizations should consider the following strategies:

Standardization: Standardize processes and procedures wherever possible to create consistency and predictability in how work is performed. Establish clear guidelines, templates, and best practices that define the "right way" to execute tasks and ensure that all employees are aligned with organizational goals and objectives.

Continuous Improvement: Foster a culture of continuous improvement that encourages employees to identify opportunities for streamlining workflows and implementing process enhancements. Provide training and support to help employees develop the skills and knowledge needed to drive ongoing innovation and excellence.

Lean Principles: Embrace Lean principles such as value stream mapping, 5S (sort, set in order, shine, standardize, sustain), and Kaizen (continuous improvement) to identify and eliminate waste in processes. Look for opportunities to reduce unnecessary movement, inventory, waiting, overproduction, and defects that add time and cost to processes without adding value.

Customer-centricity: Keep the needs and preferences of customers at the forefront of process design and optimization efforts. Solicit feedback from customers and stakeholders to understand their pain points and priorities and incorporate their input into process redesign efforts. Design processes with the end-user in mind, aiming to deliver products and services that meet or exceed customer expectations.

By streamlining workflows for optimal performance, organizations can achieve greater efficiency, agility, and customer satisfaction, enabling them to thrive in today's competitive marketplace.

This section provides insights into the process redesign phase of the Re-engineering process, emphasizing the importance of redesigning core business processes, eliminating redundancies and inefficiencies, and streamlining workflows for optimal performance. It lays the groundwork for the practical application of Re-engineering principles to enhance quality and drive organizational improvement.

CHAPTER 6:

Technology Integration

Technology integration plays a pivotal role in enhancing quality through Re-engineering, offering organizations powerful tools and capabilities to drive continuous improvement and innovation. In this section, we will explore the importance of leveraging technology for quality improvement, strategies for selecting and implementing appropriate tools, and common challenges in technology adoption and how to overcome them.

6.1 Leveraging Technology for Quality Improvement

Technology has become an indispensable enabler of quality improvement initiatives, offering organizations a wide range of tools and capabilities to streamline processes, enhance decision-making, and drive innovation. By leveraging technology effectively, organizations can achieve significant improvements in quality, efficiency, and customer satisfaction. Some ways in which technology can be leveraged for quality improvement include:

Automation: Automation involves using technology to perform repetitive tasks or processes automatically, without human intervention. By automating routine tasks, organizations can reduce the risk of errors, speed up cycle times, and free up employees to focus on more value-added activities.

Data Analytics: Data analytics involves analyzing large volumes of data to uncover patterns, trends, and insights that can inform decision-making and drive improvement efforts. By harnessing the power of data analytics, organizations can gain a deeper understanding of their processes, identify root causes of quality issues, and develop targeted solutions to address them.

Collaboration Tools: Collaboration tools enable employees to communicate, share information, and collaborate on projects in real time, regardless of their physical location. By fostering collaboration and knowledge sharing, these tools help break down silos, improve cross-functional coordination, and accelerate problem-solving and decision-making processes.

Quality Management Systems (QMS): Quality management systems are software platforms that help organizations manage and control their quality processes and documentation. QMS platforms typically include features such as document control, corrective and preventive action (CAPA) management, audit management, and compliance tracking, enabling organizations to ensure compliance with quality standards and regulations.

Internet of Things (IoT): The Internet of Things refers to the network of interconnected devices, sensors, and systems that collect and exchange data. By leveraging IoT technology, organizations can monitor and analyze real-time data from equipment, machinery, and processes to identify potential issues, optimize performance, and proactively address quality concerns.

Artificial Intelligence (AI): Artificial intelligence encompasses a range of technologies that enable machines to perform tasks that typically require human intelligence, such as problem-solving, pattern recognition, and decision-making. By harnessing the power of AI, organizations can automate complex tasks, optimize processes, and improve predictive capabilities, leading to better quality outcomes.

By embracing these technologies and incorporating them into their quality improvement efforts, organizations can achieve greater efficiency, effectiveness, and competitiveness in today's fast-paced business environment.

6.2 Selecting and Implementing Appropriate Tools

Selecting and implementing appropriate technology tools is critical to the success of quality improvement initiatives. Organizations must carefully evaluate their needs, objectives, and constraints to identify the right tools and ensure successful implementation. Some strategies for selecting and implementing appropriate tools include:

Assessing Needs and Objectives: Start by clearly defining the needs and objectives of the quality improvement initiative. What specific problems or challenges are you trying to address? What outcomes do you hope to achieve? By understanding your needs and objectives, you can identify technology tools that align with your goals and priorities.

Conducting Due Diligence: Once you have identified potential technology tools, conduct thorough research to evaluate their features, functionality, and suitability for your organization. Consider factors such as cost, scalability, ease of use, and compatibility with existing systems. Reach out to vendors for product demonstrations, case studies, and customer references to gather additional insights.

Pilot Testing: Before fully committing to a technology tool, consider conducting a pilot test to evaluate its effectiveness and suitability in a real-world setting. Select a small-scale pilot project that represents typical use cases and workflows within your organization and closely monitor the results. Solicit feedback from end-users and stakeholders to identify any issues or challenges that need to be addressed before wider implementation.

Training and Support: Provide comprehensive training and support to ensure that employees are proficient in using the technology tools effectively. Offer training sessions, workshops, and online resources to help employees develop the skills and knowledge needed to maximize the benefits of the tools. Establish channels for ongoing support and troubleshooting to address any issues or questions that arise during implementation.

Monitoring and Evaluation: Continuously monitor and evaluate the performance of the technology tools to ensure that they are delivering the expected benefits and outcomes. Track key performance indicators (KPIs) such as process efficiency, error rates, and customer satisfaction to assess the impact of the tools on quality improvement efforts. Make adjustments as needed to optimize performance and address any emerging challenges.

By following these strategies, organizations can select and implement technology tools that effectively support their quality improvement objectives and drive meaningful results.

6.3 Overcoming Challenges in Technology Adoption

While technology offers tremendous opportunities for quality improvement, organizations may encounter various challenges in the adoption and implementation of technology tools. Some common challenges and strategies for overcoming them include:

Resistance to Change: Resistance to change is a common barrier to technology adoption, as employees may be reluctant to embrace new tools or processes. To overcome resistance, involve employees in the decision-making process, communicate the benefits of the technology tools, and provide training and support to help them adapt to the changes.

Lack of Resources: Limited resources, including budget, time, and expertise, can hinder the adoption of technology tools. To overcome resource constraints, prioritize investments based on the potential impact on quality improvement objectives, explore cost-effective solutions, and leverage external resources such as consultants or technology partners to fill gaps in expertise.

Integration Challenges: Integrating new technology tools with existing systems and processes can be complex and challenging. To overcome integration challenges, carefully assess compatibility and inter-operability requirements upfront, involve IT and business stakeholders in the planning process, and develop a roadmap for phased implementation to minimize disruption and ensure a smooth transition.

Data Security and Privacy Concerns: Data security and privacy concerns may arise when implementing technology tools that involve the collection, storage, or processing of sensitive information. To address these concerns, implement robust security measures, such as encryption, access controls, and data encryption, to protect sensitive data. Ensure compliance with relevant regulations and standards, such as GDPR or HIPAA, and communicate transparently with stakeholders about data handling practices.

Limited Technical Expertise: Limited technical expertise within the organization can pose challenges in the adoption and implementation of technology tools. To overcome this challenge, invest in training and development programs to build technical skills among employees, leverage external expertise through partnerships or consulting services, and foster a culture of learning and experimentation that encourages employees to explore new technologies and develop their expertise.

By proactively addressing these challenges and implementing strategies to overcome them, organizations can successfully adopt and leverage technology tools to drive quality improvement initiatives and achieve sustainable results.

This section provides insights into the importance of technology integration in enhancing quality through Re-engineering, strategies for selecting and implementing appropriate tools, and common challenges in technology adoption and how to overcome them. It lays the groundwork for leveraging technology effectively to drive continuous improvement and innovation in organizational processes and practices.

CHAPTER 7:

Change Management

Change management is a critical aspect of any Re-engineering initiative, as it involves understanding the human side of change, effectively communicating with stakeholders, managing resistance, and building buy-in to ensure the success of quality improvement efforts. In this section, we will explore the importance of change management in enhancing quality through Re-engineering and provide strategies for navigating the complexities of organizational change.

7.1 Understanding the Human Side of Change

At its core, change management is about understanding the human side of change and addressing the emotional, psychological, and cultural factors that influence how people respond to change. Change can evoke a range of emotions, including fear, uncertainty, and resistance, as individuals grapple with the unknown and the prospect of leaving behind familiar ways of working. To effectively manage change, organizations must:

Empathy: Recognize and acknowledge the emotions and concerns of employees who are affected by the change. Empathize with their perspectives and experiences, and demonstrate a willingness to listen and address their needs and concerns.

Communication: Establish open and transparent communication channels to keep employees informed and engaged throughout the change process. Provide regular updates on the reasons for the change, its potential impact, and the steps being taken to support employees through the transition.

Involvement: Involve employees in the change process by soliciting their input, feedback, and ideas for improvement. Encourage participation in decision-making and problem-solving activities to foster a sense of ownership and empowerment.

Support: Provide support and resources to help employees adapt to the change and overcome any challenges or obstacles they may encounter. Offer training, coaching, and counseling services to help employees develop the skills and resilience needed to navigate change successfully.

By understanding the human side of change and addressing the emotional and psychological aspects of the transition, organizations can create a supportive environment that enables employees to embrace change and contribute to its success.

7.2 Communicating Effectively with Stakeholders

Effective communication is essential for successful change management, as it helps build trust, alignment, and commitment among stakeholders. When communicating about the Re-engineering initiative, organizations should:

Be Transparent: Be transparent about the reasons for the change, its potential impact, and the expected outcomes. Provide clear and honest information to stakeholders, and address any concerns or questions openly and honestly.

Tailor Messages: The Tailor communicates messages to different stakeholder groups based on their needs, preferences, and level of involvement in the change process. Use language and examples that resonate with each audience, and emphasize the relevance and importance of the change to their roles and responsibilities.

Use Multiple Channels: Use multiple communication channels to reach different stakeholder groups and ensure that key messages are effectively conveyed. Utilize a combination of face-to-face meetings, email updates, intranet announcements, and other communication tools to reach a diverse audience.

Provide Feedback Mechanisms: Establish feedback mechanisms to solicit input, feedback, and questions from stakeholders throughout the change process. Encourage open dialogue and active participation, and respond promptly to any concerns or issues raised by stakeholders.

By communicating effectively with stakeholders, organizations can build trust, credibility, and support for the Re-engineering initiative, increasing the likelihood of its success.

7.3 Managing Resistance and Building Buy-in

Resistance to change is a natural and common response, as individuals may feel threatened by the uncertainty and disruption that change can bring. To effectively manage resistance and build buy-in for the Re-engineering initiative, organizations should:

Anticipate Resistance: Anticipate potential sources of resistance to change and proactively address them before they escalate. Identify key stakeholders who may be resistant to the change and develop strategies to engage them and address their concerns.

Communicate the Benefits: Communicate the benefits of the Re-engineering initiative and how it aligns with the organization's goals and objectives. Highlight the positive impact that the change will have on employees, customers, and other stakeholders, and emphasize the opportunities for growth and development that it presents.

Provide Support: Provide support and resources to help employees navigate the change and overcome any challenges or obstacles they may encounter. Offer training, coaching, and counseling services to help employees develop the skills and resilience needed to adapt to the new ways of working.

Celebrate Successes: Celebrate successes and milestones along the way to reinforce progress and momentum. Recognize and reward employees who embrace the change contribute to its success, and share success stories and best practices to inspire others.

By actively managing resistance and building buy-in for the Re-engineering initiative, organizations can create a culture of change readiness and agility that enables them to adapt and thrive in today's dynamic business environment.

This section provides insights into the importance of change management in enhancing quality through Re-engineering, emphasizing the need to understand the human side of change, communicate effectively with stakeholders, and manage resistance while building buy-in for the Re-engineering initiative. It lays the groundwork for successful change implementation and adoption, enabling organizations to achieve their quality improvement goals effectively.

CHAPTER 8:

Continuous Improvement

Continuous improvement is a foundational principle of Re-engineering, emphasizing the need for organizations to continually strive for excellence and innovation in their processes, products, and services. In this section, we will explore the importance of continuous improvement, strategies for establishing feedback mechanisms for continuous learning, monitoring key performance indicators (KPIs), and implementing iterative improvement cycles for sustained results.

8.1 Establishing Feedback Mechanisms for Continuous Learning

Feedback mechanisms are essential for facilitating continuous learning and improvement within organizations. By gathering feedback from employees, customers, and other stakeholders, organizations can identify opportunities for enhancement, address issues and challenges, and drive ongoing innovation. Some strategies for establishing feedback mechanisms for continuous learning include:

Employee Feedback: Encourage employees to provide feedback on their experiences, challenges, and suggestions for improvement. Implement regular surveys, suggestion boxes, or open-door policies to gather input from employees at all levels of the organization. Create a culture that values and rewards feedback, and actively solicit input from employees on ways to enhance processes, systems, and practices.

Customer Feedback: Solicit feedback from customers on their experiences with products, services, and interactions with the organization. Use surveys, focus groups, and customer satisfaction scores to gather insights into customer preferences, pain points, and areas for improvement. Analyze customer feedback to identify trends, patterns, and opportunities for enhancing quality and delivering superior value.

Supplier Feedback: Engage with suppliers and partners to gather feedback on their experiences and interactions with the organization. Build relationships based on trust and collaboration, and encourage open communication to identify opportunities for process optimization, cost reduction, and quality enhancement. Use supplier feedback to improve supplier performance, strengthen partnerships, and drive mutual success.

Performance Reviews: Conduct regular performance reviews to evaluate the effectiveness of processes, systems, and practices and identify areas for improvement. Use key performance indicators (KPIs) to track performance against objectives and benchmarks, and analyze performance data to identify trends, patterns, and areas of under-performance. Use performance reviews as an opportunity to celebrate successes, recognize achievements, and identify opportunities for enhancement.

By establishing feedback mechanisms for continuous learning, organizations can create a culture of continuous improvement and innovation that enables them to adapt and thrive in today's dynamic business environment.

8.2 Monitoring Key Performance Indicators (KPIs)

Key performance indicators (KPIs) are critical metrics that organizations use to measure progress toward their goals and objectives. By monitoring KPIs, organizations can identify trends, track performance, and make data-driven decisions to drive continuous improvement. Some common KPIs used in quality improvement initiatives include:

Quality Metrics: Quality metrics measure the effectiveness and efficiency of processes, products, and services in meeting customer requirements and expectations. Examples of quality metrics include defect rates, customer satisfaction scores, on-time delivery performance, and process cycle times. By monitoring quality metrics, organizations can identify areas for improvement and implement corrective actions to enhance quality and customer satisfaction.

Operational Efficiency: Operational efficiency metrics measure the efficiency of organizational processes and resources in achieving desired outcomes. Examples of operational efficiency metrics include productivity levels, resource utilization rates, and cost per unit produced. By monitoring operational efficiency metrics, organizations can identify opportunities to streamline processes, reduce waste, and optimize resource allocation to improve efficiency and reduce costs.

Customer Satisfaction: Customer satisfaction metrics measure the satisfaction levels of customers with products, services, and interactions with the organization. Examples of customer satisfaction metrics include Net Promoter Score (NPS), customer retention rates, and customer feedback scores. By monitoring customer satisfaction metrics, organizations can identify areas for improvement and take proactive measures to enhance the customer experience and build customer loyalty.

Employee Engagement: Employee engagement metrics measure the level of engagement and satisfaction of employees with their work and the organization. Examples of employee engagement metrics include employee turnover rates, employee satisfaction scores, and employee feedback scores. By monitoring employee engagement metrics, organizations can identify factors that impact employee morale and productivity and take steps to create a positive work environment that fosters engagement and performance.

By monitoring key performance indicators (KPIs) related to quality, efficiency, customer satisfaction, and employee engagement, organizations can gain valuable insights into their performance and make informed decisions to drive continuous improvement and achieve their quality improvement goals.

8.3 Iterative Improvement Cycles for Sustained Results

Iterative improvement cycles are a fundamental aspect of continuous improvement, enabling organizations to implement changes, measure their impact, and adjust courses based on feedback and results. By adopting an iterative approach to improvement, organizations can:

Plan: Define objectives, goals, and targets for improvement initiatives based on strategic priorities and organizational needs. Establish clear metrics and benchmarks to measure progress and success.

Implement: Implement changes and initiatives designed to achieve improvement objectives. Communicate changes effectively to stakeholders and provide training and support to ensure successful implementation.

Measure: Monitor performance against key performance indicators (KPIs) to assess the impact of changes and initiatives. Gather feedback from stakeholders and evaluate results to identify areas of success and areas for improvement.

Adjust: Based on feedback and results, make adjustments to processes, practices, and initiatives to optimize performance and achieve desired outcomes. Continuously iterate and refine improvement efforts to drive sustained results over time.

By embracing iterative improvement cycles, organizations can foster a culture of experimentation, learning, and adaptation that enables them to respond effectively to changing conditions and continuously improve their processes, products, and services.

This section provides insights into the importance of continuous improvement in enhancing quality through Re-engineering, emphasizing the need for establishing feedback mechanisms for continuous learning, monitoring key performance indicators (KPIs), and implementing iterative improvement cycles for sustained results. It lays the groundwork for driving ongoing innovation and excellence in organizational processes and practices, enabling organizations to achieve their quality improvement goals effectively.

Priscilla Knox

CHAPTER 9:

Case Studies

In this section, we will explore real-world examples of successful Re-engineering projects that have resulted in significant enhancements in quality and performance. Through these case studies, we will examine the challenges faced, strategies employed, lessons learned, and best practices adopted by organizations to achieve their quality improvement goals.

9.1 Real-world Examples of Successful Re-engineering Projects

Case Study 1: Company X - Streamlining Manufacturing Processes

Company X, a leading manufacturer in the automotive industry, embarked on a Re-engineering initiative to streamline its manufacturing processes and enhance product quality. The company faced challenges such as inefficient production workflows, high defect rates, and long lead times, which impacting customer satisfaction and profitability.

To address these challenges, Company X implemented a series of Re-engineering measures, including:

Process Mapping: Conducted a comprehensive analysis of existing manufacturing processes to identify inefficiencies, bottlenecks, and areas for improvement. Used process mapping techniques to visualize workflows and pinpoint opportunities for streamlining.

Automation: Invested in advanced automation technologies, such as robotics and machine learning, to automate repetitive tasks, reduce manual labor, and improve production efficiency. Implemented automated quality control systems to detect defects in real time and minimize scrap and rework.

Cross-Functional Collaboration: Fostered collaboration between different departments and functions to break down silos and improve communication and coordination. Implemented cross-functional teams to tackle complex problems and drive continuous improvement initiatives.

Employee Training and Empowerment: Provided extensive training and development opportunities to employees to enhance their skills and knowledge. Empowered frontline workers to identify and address quality issues proactively, fostering a culture of ownership and accountability.

As a result of these Re-engineering efforts, Company X achieved significant improvements in quality, efficiency, and customer satisfaction. Defect rates decreased by 30%, lead times were reduced by 40%, and production throughput increased by 20%. The company's reputation for quality and reliability improved, leading to increased market share and revenue growth.

Case Study 2: Hospital Y - Optimizing Patient Care Processes

Hospital Y, a large healthcare facility, undertook a Re-engineering initiative to optimize patient care processes and improve healthcare outcomes. The hospital faced challenges such as long wait times, inefficient resource allocation, and inconsistent quality of care, which were impacting patient satisfaction and clinical outcomes.

To address these challenges, Hospital Y implemented a series of Re-engineering measures, including:

Patient Flow Analysis: Conducted a thorough analysis of patient flow through the hospital, from admission to discharge, to identify bottlenecks, delays, and inefficiencies. Used data analytics tools to analyze patient data and identify patterns and trends.

Redesigning Care Pathways: Redesigned care pathways and treatment protocols to standardize care delivery, reduce variation, and improve consistency and quality. Implemented evidence-based practices and clinical guidelines to ensure that patients received appropriate and timely care.

Technology Integration: Leveraged technology solutions, such as electronic health records (EHRs) and telemedicine platforms, to streamline communication, enhance collaboration, and improve access to information. Implemented remote monitoring systems to track patient progress and intervene proactively when necessary.

Patient Engagement: Engaged patients and their families in the care process, soliciting their input, preferences, and feedback to personalize care and improve satisfaction. Implemented patient education programs and support services to empower patients to take an active role in managing their health.

As a result of these Re-engineering efforts, Hospital Y achieved significant improvements in patient satisfaction, clinical outcomes, and operational efficiency. Wait times decreased by 50%, length of stay decreased by 20%, and patient readmission rates decreased by 15%. The hospital's reputation for quality care and patient-centeredness improved, leading to increased referrals and revenue growth.

9.2 Lessons Learned and Best Practices

From these case studies, several key lessons and best practices emerge for organizations embarking on Re-engineering initiatives to enhance quality:

Leadership Commitment: Strong leadership commitment and support are essential for driving Re-engineering initiatives and overcoming resistance to change.

Cross-Functional Collaboration: Foster collaboration between different departments and functions to break down silos and harness collective expertise and insights.

Data-Driven Decision-Making: Use data analytics and performance metrics to inform decision-making and measure the impact of Re-engineering efforts.

Continuous Improvement: Embrace a culture of continuous improvement and innovation, encouraging employees to challenge the status quo and seek opportunities for enhancement.

Customer-centricity: Place a strong emphasis on understanding and meeting the needs and preferences of customers, tailoring products and services to deliver superior value.

Employee Engagement: Empower and engage employees in the change process, soliciting their input, feedback, and ideas for improvement.

Iterative Approach: Adopt an iterative approach to improvement, implementing changes incrementally and adjusting courses based on feedback and results.

By applying these lessons and best practices, organizations can increase the likelihood of success and achieve sustainable improvements in quality, performance, and customer satisfaction through Re-engineering.

This section provides insights into real-world examples of successful Re-engineering projects, highlighting the challenges faced, strategies employed, lessons learned, and best practices adopted by organizations to enhance quality and performance. It offers valuable lessons and inspiration for organizations embarking on Re-engineering initiatives of their own, guiding them toward effective implementation and sustainable results.

CHAPTER 10:

Future Trends and Considerations

As organizations continue to evolve and adapt to a rapidly changing business landscape, it's essential to anticipate future trends and considerations in quality management and Re-engineering. In this section, we will explore emerging trends, potential challenges, and opportunities that may shape the future of enhancing quality through Re-engineering.

10.1 Emerging Trends in Quality Management and Re-engineering

Digital Transformation: The ongoing digital transformation is revolutionizing how organizations approach quality management and Re-engineering. Technologies such as artificial intelligence, machine learning, and the Internet of Things (IoT) are being increasingly integrated into processes to drive efficiency, predictability, and agility.

Data Analytics and Predictive Analytics: Data analytics and predictive analytics are becoming indispensable tools for quality management and Re-engineering. Organizations are leveraging data to gain insights into their processes, identify trends, and predict future outcomes, enabling them to make data-driven decisions and anticipate issues before they arise.

Customer-centricity: Customer-centricity is emerging as a key focus area for quality management and Re-engineering. Organizations are placing greater emphasis on understanding and meeting the needs and preferences of customers, tailoring products and services to deliver personalized experiences and enhance customer satisfaction.

Agile and Lean Practices: Agile and lean practices are gaining traction in quality management and Re-engineering, enabling organizations to respond more quickly to changing market dynamics and customer requirements. Agile methodologies such as Scrum and Kanban are being applied to Re-engineering efforts to foster collaboration, flexibility, and innovation.

Sustainability and Social Responsibility: Sustainability and social responsibility are increasingly influencing quality management and Re-engineering initiatives. Organizations are incorporating environmental, social, and governance (ESG) considerations into their processes, products, and practices, aiming to minimize their environmental footprint and create positive social impact.

10.2 Anticipating Challenges and Opportunities

Technological Disruption: Technological disruption presents both challenges and opportunities for quality management and Re-engineering. While technology offers the potential to drive significant improvements in quality and performance, organizations must navigate the complexities of implementing and integrating new technologies into existing processes and systems.

Globalization and Supply Chain Complexity: Globalization and supply chain complexity are posing challenges for quality management and Re-engineering. As supply chains become increasingly interconnected and geographically dispersed, organizations must manage risks related to quality control, supplier performance, and regulatory compliance across diverse markets and regions.

Changing Regulatory Landscape: The changing regulatory landscape presents challenges for quality management and Re-engineering, as organizations must stay abreast of evolving regulations and standards. Compliance with regulations such as ISO standards, FDA requirements, and industry-specific regulations requires organizations to maintain robust quality management systems and practices.

Talent Acquisition and Retention: Talent acquisition and retention are critical considerations for quality management and Re-engineering. Organizations must attract and retain skilled professionals with expertise in data analytics, process optimization, and change management to drive successful Re-engineering initiatives and sustain quality improvements over time.

Cultural Resistance to Change: Cultural resistance to change can hinder quality management and Re-engineering efforts, as employees may be reluctant to embrace new processes, technologies, or ways of working. Organizations must invest in change management strategies to address resistance, foster a culture of innovation and continuous improvement, and empower employees to adapt to change effectively.

Conclusion

As organizations navigate the complexities of enhancing quality through Re-engineering, it's essential to anticipate future trends and considerations that may shape the landscape. By embracing emerging trends, addressing challenges, and seizing opportunities, organizations can position themselves for success and achieve sustainable improvements in quality, performance, and customer satisfaction in the years to come.

This section provides insights into future trends and considerations in quality management and Re-engineering, highlighting emerging trends, potential challenges, and opportunities that organizations may encounter as they strive to enhance quality through Re-engineering. It offers valuable guidance for organizations seeking to stay ahead of the curve and drive continuous improvement and innovation in their processes, products, and practices.

Priscilla Knox

CHAPTER 11:

Conclusion

In this comprehensive guide, we have explored the principles, strategies, and practices involved in enhancing quality through Re-engineering. From understanding the concept of Re-engineering to implementing iterative improvement cycles, we have covered a wide range of topics aimed at helping organizations drive continuous improvement and innovation in their processes, products, and services. As we conclude this guide, let's recap some key insights and reflect on the importance of enhancing quality through Re-engineering.

11.1 Recap of Key Insights

Foundations of Quality: Quality is a fundamental aspect of organizational success, encompassing both product quality and process quality. By focusing on improving quality, organizations can enhance customer satisfaction, increase operational efficiency, and drive competitive advantage.

The Re-engineering Approach: Re-engineering involves radical redesign and improvement of processes to achieve significant enhancements in quality, performance, and customer satisfaction.

By challenging existing assumptions and embracing innovative solutions, organizations can achieve breakthrough results through Re-engineering.

Change Management: Change management is critical for the success of Re-engineering initiatives, as it involves understanding the human side of change, communicating effectively with stakeholders, managing resistance, and building buy-in. By fostering a culture of change readiness and agility, organizations can navigate the complexities of organizational change and drive successful Re-engineering efforts.

Continuous Improvement: Continuous improvement is essential for sustaining quality enhancements over time. By establishing feedback mechanisms for continuous learning, monitoring key performance indicators (KPIs), and implementing iterative improvement cycles, organizations can drive ongoing innovation and excellence in their processes, products, and services.

Technology Integration: Technology plays a pivotal role in enhancing quality through Re-engineering, offering organizations powerful tools and capabilities to streamline processes, improve decision-making, and drive innovation. By leveraging technology effectively, organizations can achieve greater efficiency, effectiveness, and competitiveness in today's fast-paced business environment.

Future Trends and Considerations: Anticipating future trends and considerations is essential for staying ahead of the curve and driving continuous improvement and innovation. By embracing emerging trends, addressing challenges, and seizing opportunities, organizations can position themselves for success and achieve sustainable improvements in quality, performance, and customer satisfaction.

11.2 Final Thoughts on Enhancing Quality Through Re-engineering

Enhancing quality through Re-engineering is not just a one-time initiative; it's a journey of continuous improvement and innovation. It requires a commitment to challenging the status quo, embracing change, and striving for excellence in everything we do. By fostering a culture of continuous learning, collaboration, and adaptation, organizations can drive meaningful change and achieve their quality improvement goals.

As we embark on this journey, it's essential to remember that enhancing quality through Re-engineering is not without its challenges. It requires dedication, perseverance, and a willingness to confront obstacles head-on. But the rewards are well worth the effort – improved customer satisfaction, increased operational efficiency, and sustained competitive advantage.

In conclusion, enhancing quality through Re-engineering is not just about making incremental improvements; it's about fundamentally transforming the way we do business to achieve breakthrough results. By embracing the principles, strategies, and practices outlined in this guide, organizations can unleash their full potential and achieve excellence in quality and performance.

Thank you for embarking on this journey with us. May your efforts to enhance quality through Re-engineering bring you success, fulfillment, and prosperity in the years to come.

This conclusion section summarizes the key insights covered in the guide and offers final thoughts on the importance of enhancing quality through Re-engineering. It emphasizes the journey of continuous improvement and innovation and encourages organizations to embrace change and strive for excellence in their quality improvement efforts.

11.3 Future Trends and Considerations

As organizations change and adapt to a quickly changing business environment, it is critical to predict future trends and considerations in quality management and Re-engineering. This section will look at developing trends, potential difficulties, and possibilities that may define the future of quality improvement through Re-engineering.

11.4 Emerging trends in quality management and Re-engineering

Digital Transformation: The continuing digital transformation is changing the way firms approach quality management and Re-engineering. Artificial intelligence, machine learning, and the Internet of Things (IoT) are increasingly being used to improve process efficiency, predictability, and agility.

Data analytics and predictive analytics are becoming important tools for quality management and Re-engineering. Organizations use data to acquire insights into their operations, spot trends, and forecast future outcomes, allowing them to make data-driven decisions and foresee problems before they occur.

Customer-centricity is becoming a critical emphasis area for quality management and Re-engineering. Organizations are putting more emphasis on knowing and matching the requirements and preferences of their customers, adapting products and services to provide personalized experiences, and increasing customer satisfaction.

Agile and Lean methods: Agile and lean methods are gaining popularity in quality management and Re-engineering, allowing businesses to adjust more swiftly to changing market dynamics and consumer needs. Agile approaches like as Scrum and Kanban are being used in Re-engineering projects to promote cooperation, adaptability, and innovation.

Sustainability and social responsibility are becoming increasingly important in quality management and Re-engineering programs. Organizations are incorporating environmental, social, and governance (ESG) issues into their processes, products, and practices to reduce their environmental footprint while also creating good social effects.

11.5 Anticipating Challenges and Opportunities

Technological disruption creates both obstacles and opportunities for quality management and Re-engineering. While technology has the potential to significantly improve quality and performance, companies must manage the complexity of introducing and integrating new technologies into existing processes and systems.

Globalization and supply chain complexity present obstacles to quality management and Re-engineering. As supply chains grow more interconnected and geographically distributed, firms must manage risks associated with quality control, supplier performance, and regulatory compliance across several markets and countries.

The changing regulatory landscape poses problems for quality management and Re-engineering, as firms must keep up with new regulations and requirements. To comply with laws like as ISO standards, FDA requirements, and industry-specific restrictions, firms must maintain strong quality management systems and practices.

Talent acquisition and retention are significant factors in quality management and Re-engineering. To drive successful Re-engineering programs and sustain long-term quality gains, organizations must attract and retain skilled personnel with expertise in data analytics, process optimization, and change management.

Cultural resistance to change can impede quality management and Re-engineering initiatives because employees may be hesitant to adopt new methods, technology, or ways of working. Organizations must invest in change management methods to overcome opposition, promote an innovative and continuous improvement culture, and enable workers to effectively adapt to change.

Conclusion

As organizations traverse the complexity of improving quality through Re-engineering, it is critical to foresee future trends and considerations that will impact the landscape. Organizations can position themselves for success and achieve long-term improvements in quality, performance, and customer happiness by embracing emerging trends, confronting difficulties, and capitalizing on opportunities.

This section discusses future trends and considerations in quality management and Re-engineering, focusing on developing trends, potential problems, and opportunities that companies may face as they attempt to improve quality through Re-engineering. It provides useful direction for firms looking to stay ahead of the competition by promoting continuous improvement and innovation in their processes, products, and practices.